Memoirs of The Marrying Man :

A Personal Account of Love, Life and Loss

By: Taijuan E. Gales

Table of Contents

The Dedication

I would like to dedicate this project to God first, who has been my rock, my anchor and source of all things my power and light. Thank you for every lesson, every ounce of patience, grace and mercy. This would not be possible without You.

I would also like to dedicate this writing to my big brother Ronald West Jr. I am often reminded of our bond, the laughs we shared and the brotherhood we forged during your time on Earth. Your legacy lives on through your beautiful family: Wife Shelly West, James West, Ronique West and Shilron West. Thank you for all the laughs, the prayers and support you always gave me. You are truly missed my brother, rest well...

Special Acknowledgements

Thank you to the family and friends that supported this project from day one. There were many days I wanted to throw in the towel and God would send a reminder to hang in there and stay the course. Much love and many thanks again.

To my mother Sherri Gales, Thank you for unconditional love and many prayers. Thank you for your direction, correction and sacrifice. Raising a young man as a single mother is one of the toughest jobs on the planet and you did a great job with the tools and knowledge you had available. Thank you for being my first inspiration and example of excellence. You are appreciated... Love you.

To my father, Ronald Jackson. Thank you for the few moments that we shared while you were here on Earth. Though I wish we had spent more time together, I value and treasure the times we did share. All I ever wanted to do was get to know you so that I could in turn get to know myself. Family and friends that knew you tell me that we're a lot alike and now that I'm at an age where I can process that information from the stories they tell and what I've come to know about myself, I take that as a compliment.

Rest well Dad… Love you always.

To my Grandmother, Annie Price. It's been said that the bond between grandparent and grandchild is a special one, and I can certainly attest to that. Thank you Grandma for all your love, prayer and support. As early as I can remember, you always taught me to pray, pray when I'm up, pray when I'm down, pray when I'm coming and pray when I'm going… You are truly the cornerstone of our family and I wanted to take a moment to honor you for being such an awesome example.

I love you.

To my Sister, Tantelya Gales. I've watched you grow from little girl, to young woman to grown woman and I am proud to call you my sister. Thank you for your love and support always. Thank you for loving me when it wasn't so easy to love me. Thank you for your many prayers. God has something very special lined up for you and I know you're ready to receive and go to the next level in life. Love you and appreciate you.

To my three beautiful children: Ra'naa, Savion, Madison. The three lights of my life... My deepest prayer is that I'm able to pass on the lessons I've learn without passing on the pain that I had to endure learning those lessons. My prayer is that I carried the cross of failed relationships so that you wouldn't have to and that all of you will healthy, happy, successful relationships. I also pray that when you read this project you will gain a better understanding of me, and that you learn a few valuable things to apply to your lives. I love you all more than words can ever express, you have been and are my inspiration.

Love you.

To Music

There were many days when music was the only thing that kept me
on track:

Go-Go - Defined the sound of my city

R & B - Inspired Late nights and Early Morning

Old School - Instilled Substance and Soul

Hip Hop - Gave me the voice I never had

Gospel - Provided Hope and Inspiration

Jazz - Gave me peace and a great appreciation for instruments

To Cinema

There are a few movies that inspired and encouraged me to write this story. Thank you to the writers, directors, producers and actors, etc. that made these films possible:

Love Jones | Dead Presidents | The Wood | The Best Man | Boyz N Da Hood | Love & Basketball | Brown Sugar | House Party | School Days | Boomerang | ATL | Do the Right Thing | Why Did I Get Married

Preface

The initial draft of this project dates back about 10 years. I would work on it, put it down and even throw it away, only having to start again from the drawing board. After throwing it away for the last time, it finally dawned on me that I had a little more "living" to do before the project could be completed.

I often thought to myself, who would care? Who would want to read about my problems, challenges and struggles? People have their own issues and lives to navigate. As I thought about it, my initial writings were coming from a place of frustration and pain. There wasn't much victory in reading what was drafted because I was still in the midst of living through my situation(s).

Now that I'm out of those situations and I have clarity and focus, I can write a project that would help someone. In having lived through four (4) marriages, I've acquired some real data that can be turned into powerful information if applied correctly.

By no means do I claim to be an expert on love and marriage, not by far. But what I can pass on is 40 years of knowledge from an African American man that believes in the power of love.

How does this book differ from other books on the market? In these writings you get the truest accounts of my life as they happened. I leave no stone unturned, no topic untouched. This is the good, the bad and the ugly of my life, unfiltered. Transparency is key when sharing information that is so close and personal.

Prayerfully, this project will help some women understand men a little better, it will give men the voice we sometimes silence for many reasons and I hope that it helps someone's marriage in the process.

Many thanks again for your purchase. I hope that it is a blessing to you in some regard.

God Bless.

The names of the women that I refer to in this project have been altered for confidentiality.

Chapter I: The Early Years

The year is 1974, a gallon of gas cost you $0.55, milk was $1.50 a gallon and Barry White's "Can't get enough of your love, babe" was topping the charts and peace and love was in the air...

I grew up on A Street, NE in my Grandmother's house. Grandma's house was the family's house. My Great grandmother, aunts, uncles, and cousins all lived there at some point. I was the first grandchild and baby of the house, and noticeably spoiled. I was the only grandchild until my little sister was born, when I was 7. I remember the age 7 well, because my cousin Trisa and I had a birthday party that year. My birthday was July 7 and her birthday was July 13, so we celebrated our birthdays together. It was my most memorable birthday because of the success of our party. There were so many family and friends present and I felt so celebrated, I felt so loved.

I had plenty of uncles, but their presence weren't as prominent as that of my mother, grandmothers and aunts. My disposition as a child was non-confrontational; I was very friendly and easy going. My first confrontational encounter was "Nu Nu", Nu Nu was known to take other's belongings and he was very intimidating. For the first time that I could remember, I felt powerlessness, like I didn't have a voice. He wanted my belongings and I didn't want to fight over them, so I just let him take them. So for a long time, I hid things or didn't take things outside because I didn't want Nu Nu to take my things. At around the age of 9, I had my first fist fight. Reggie was notorious for being a fighter. As I was walking home from school, I noticed Reggie and immediately switched sides of the street to avoid him. He approached me and tried to fight me and I ran home. When I got home, my mother asked me why I was out of breath. She said I know you didn't run in the house away from a fight. She asked why he was chasing me and told me that if I didn't beat Reggie up, that I would have to fight her. The bottled up emotion from avoiding confrontation with Nu Nu fueled my energy in the fight with Reggie and I won.

That following summer, I went to stay with my Dad. I had spent very little time with him and I was elated to spend the entire summer with him. It was me, Dad, my Dad's girlfriend and my little sister. He owned a car detailing shop and one day he was cleaning a Mercedes Benz and that is where my fascination with the German automobiles began. He was very detailed and he cared a lot about his work which always stuck with me.

One night after dinner, I asked for money to go to the store. He gave me a $5 dollar bill and I went to the store. I made my purchase and was on my way home, when a group of neighborhood kids approached me and asked me for my treats from the store and I ran because it was a group of them.

For the second time, I felt helpless afraid as I ran to my father's house. I had a talk with my Dad about the situation and because he was well respected in the neighborhood, my Dad took me to outside to talk to the young men in the neighborhood and from that day until the end of my stay and they never bothered me again. That is the first time that I saw how strong my father really was and felt his protection.

When I returned home from the summer with my Dad, my mother informed me that we would be moving out of Grandma's house. I had mixed emotions about moving. This would mean that I wouldn't be around my family, which I would have to attend a new school, live in a new neighborhood, and make new friends. After a year of working hard and saving, we packed up and moved to our new neighborhood.

Chapter II: The Transition | Junior High School | The Story of Alicia

The move to Paradise Housing Community was strange, yet familiar. It was strange because we moved from a three level row house in a neighborhood to a 2 bedroom apartment in a complex, and familiar because I had family that lived in Paradise that would visit my grandmother's house. My aunt Ruth, my cousin Donald, my cousin Trisa, my cousin Reinard, the Boozers, would always visit my grandmother's house. They welcomed us to the neighborhood and let us know that if we needed anything, that they were just a telephone call away. Another odd feeling was becoming the man of the house. At least at my grandmother's house, I had cousins and uncles that had filled that role, but now it's just me and I have to protect my mother and my sister by any means necessary.

With a 7 year age difference between my sister and I, we got along but we didn't get along. Because my mom worked a lot, I had to baby sit my sister pretty often. This instilled a responsibility that will stick with me until this day. It was sometimes frustrating, because when I wanted to go outside, I had to be the big brother. If I wanted to participate in an extra-curricular activity, I had to be big brother and take my sister along with me. I wanted to help my mother as much as I could without being an additional burden but I also wanted to just be a kid. I wanted to enjoy the same freedom to come and go as other kids.

In addition to the change in environment, I had to adapt to a few other elements that I wasn't used to. Instead of there being 2 bullies in the neighborhood, there was a whole gang of them. There wasn't much drug culture in my grandmother's neighborhood, but it was prevalent in this environment. I remember my mother having a very serious talk with me about drugs and gangs violence. She told me about the effects of drugs, and the likely results of gang culture. I stayed as far away from them both as best I could.

I spent a lot of time with the Boozer's and at my Aunt Ruth's house. My cousin Donald, who went to Eastern Senior High School, was one of my favorite older cousins and probably my first role model. My cousin Reinard was a few years older than me, but was always cool and dressed very nice. My cousin Trisa was the same age as me, so she knew all the kids in the neighborhood that were in our age range. She introduced me to new people, which was great because I didn't have to prove myself. In a lot of neighborhoods in DC, if you don't know someone or are related to someone, you have to prove yourself, which likely meant fighting.

After the summer I spent with my dad, I didn't hear much from him and it weighed on me heavy. My mother would often try to talk to me, but I would often shut down because I would get so emotional. My mother decided to be proactive and sought out the services of the Big Brother and Big Sister mentoring program. My Big Brothers name was John. John was an old gentleman with a wife and older daughter. I remember him always dressing really nice in a suit and driving a nice car. Though he wasn't a replacement for my dad, he was a really good addition to my life. During that time in my life, like most kids in that era, The Cosby Show was a really big influence on my life. It showed black people educated, doing well, and raising a family. For as far back as I can remember, that's all I wanted to do. Growing up without a father usually has one of two results: you either end up following in those footstep or you choose you own path. I wanted to be a father that was there for kids just like Bill Cosby. I was smart enough to know and understand a television show from reality, but the show provided an excellent template for having a successful family. While the rest of the guy my age would claim to be the character Theo Huxtable, I would always claim the character Cliff Huxtable. I chose Cliff because he was a successful doctor married to the beautiful Clair Huxtable who was a lawyer and she was a great mother. Cliff also gave great advice and taught lessons in the most subtle and comical ways.

With this move to Paradise, there also came a move to a new elementary school. So I left Gibbs Elementary School and moved onto Neval Thomas Elementary. A lot of my new neighbors and friends attended Neval Thomas so that was half the battle fought. The other battle was being able to adapt to the teaching styles of these new instructors since everyone relays information differently. My new teachers turned out to be really good so that also helped with the transition. One particular teacher I took a liking to was the art teacher, Mr. Boone.

With dad's absence, there was a void that needed to be filled with something constructive. I loved music a lot and I ventured into drawing as an outlet. I would start off tracing my favorite comic book characters and soon start to create my own.

One day Mr. Boone announced that there would be an art contest at the school sponsored by DC Public Schools and Disney. The art contest consisted of a drawing of a Disney character and a quote or slogan that would promote the importance of learning and studying.

I went home excited about the contest and told my mom. She was in the kitchen cooking at the time when I mentioned the contest and she looked at me and said "DC Public Schools don't give away those types of trips" and went back to cooking.

Determined not to let her opinion or comments deter me, I worked with Mr. Boone on my concept and execution. We came up with a concept for Mickey Mouse to cook up this formula for learning and studying. So Mickey was standing in a Chef's outfit, holding a wooden spoon. From the pot, he was brewing up some elements that are included in developing better learning and study habits.

A couple weeks passed and the results came back from the drawing contest, I won first place. The First place prize was an all-expenses paid trip for four to Disney World in Orlando Florida. I rushed home to tell my mom I had won the contest and she didn't believe me. She wanted to see it in writing before she got too excited. A few weeks after winning the contest, there was a banquet held for all the winners. By this time, she believed me. I'm laughing to myself as I type this because all I can see is my mom with her shades on strutting through the airport like a superstar. If was funnier because she didn't even believe any of it would happen. I decided to take my mom, my sister and my Grandmother on the trip to Florida. It was one of my best childhood memories and proudest. I was proud because I made it happen. Something I did put a smile on my mother's face and it didn't cost her a thing. She always worked really hard to make sure we had all the necessities in life. If felt good to give her a break.

After graduating Neval Thomas Elementary, I went onto Carter G. Woodson Junior High School. At this point I'm moving into the next phase in my life. I'm starting to care more about my appearance, music, being cool, etc. Also around this time I started to really notice what was going on in the city, in reference to the drug culture and what came with it. I knew there was a lot of money, cars, clothes and women involved but never really connected the dots on how it all came to be. I knew you sold something to make a profit and that was about it. It wasn't until a conversation I had with a close friend and cousin about how the game really worked that I understand it, all of it. You don't necessarily have to be a part of a thing to understand a thing.

My mother warned me as soon as we moved in that any involvement in the drug culture and "that life" had consequences. She told me not only would I be in trouble with the law, I had to deal with her as well. My mother's voice and temper at that time in my life was enough to scare me straight.

One of the bi-product of the game was making money. Money enabled you to buy clothes, which is why a lot of guys I knew hustled. They wanted to stay fresh to impress the girls and it was bragging rights amongst the men. So without that type of financial backing, I had to manage what my mother was able to provide as best as possible. I had to become a master negotiator early in life to get the most for my dollar.

I remember shopping at a local clothing store, Morton's, while guys that hustled shopped at Cavaliers, Woodies, Macy's, etc. Another part of DC culture, joning also known as snapping, ranking, etc. Verbal warfare used to defame or humiliate an opponent. And because I wasn't able to shop at the more expensive stores, I either directly or indirectly became a target. Nothing is more embarrassing than having on clothes from Morton's and being joned on. So, I have to get ahead of the eight ball and learn how to jone. I didn't want to hurt people's feeling but I also didn't want to get embarrassed. So I became a wordsmith of sort and earned my rank as one of the best out of self-defense and survival.

After getting that aspect of my life under control, then came the next obstacle: Girls. I had a little girlfriend in elementary but like all relationships at that point in life it was very short lived, might have been 3 weeks. But once I got to Junior High, I knew I was in trouble. Girls were no longer girls, they were GIRLS. I wasn't one to attempt sex because of my mother's advice but still I was interested.

Music played a huge role in how I felt about love and women. My mother played a lot of Marvin Gaye, Anita Baker, Whitney Houston, Luther Vandross, etc. while cleaning the house. This music, this sound, these lyrics… I remember how all of those elements made me feel and it felt good. I listened to the love songs, the heartbreak songs, the break up songs, the get back together songs. So I got a well-rounded dose of information even though I needed an example from my parent on how to be in and maintain a relationship.

Around 8th grade, I meet Tierra. Tierra was my very first crush, a real crush. She was smart, pretty and dressed really nice. We were in the same homeroom and everyone knew about my crush on Tierra.

We had an assembly around Valentine's Day. The school hosted a secret Valentine's mail box. You could mail a secret Valentine to anyone in the school and they would deliver the Valentine to your person of choice. You had to tape a penny to it for postage.

During the assembly, the school made announcements and gave out awards. During an intermission, they started to hand out the secret Valentine's. Tierra received my secret Valentine. Because of the popularity of my drawing talents, people could figure out who it was from. She smiled and turned around and thanked me. Right after that, someone snatched the card from her and passed it around. I was so embarrassed for a few reasons. First because of what I said in the letter. Don't remember it verbatim but I did draw a picture of Mickey and Minnie Mouse holding a huge heart. That trip to Disney really inspired some things. Second, after the assembly Tierra and I had a conversation. She was really appreciative of the secret

Valentine but she let me know that she had a boyfriend. So my first real crush became my first heartbreak.

That next year, I was eligible to work for the Mayor Marion Barry Summer Youth Program. It would be my first job. It was an Architects training course at Howard University. This summer job meant a lot to me because it meant that I could earn my own money to shop for my own clothes. I was too excited. But my mother brought me back to reality very fast. She informed me that after the first two weeks I would have to now budget for my Metro expenses back and forth to work and lunch money in addition to trying to stay fresh. She was helping me to become responsible and accountable for what I earned early in life.

So like most kids in the city around that time, I became a sneaker head. I bought my first pair of Jordans with my first paycheck. I was broke again right after that purchase. I was happy for the moment but still had to make it back and forth to work, eat lunch, etc. I didn't like that feeling at all. Learning to manage my money became important to me after that.

So now that I was dressing a little better, equipped to handle and protect myself, and just got over my first heartbreak. I was feeling better about myself as a person but still knew I lacked a lot of the key elements for becoming a man. So as a result of going through all of these displaced emotions, I started to act out and play too much in school. My academics took a pretty big hit around 9th grade and I started bringing home poor progress reports and failing classes. As a result, my mother decided to put me on punishment for an entire summer break. From June when school let out until September when school opens back up. So we're talking an entire summer of studying, cleaning and understanding why academics are so important to life. I was excited to take the trash outside. It was a tough lesson to learn but I'm thankful for it today.

By the time I start to get my grades back up to standard, it's time for me to choose a high school to go to. I wanted to attend Eastern Senior High School for a few reasons. As I was leaving junior high, Tierra and I decided to remain friends and stay in touch. She decided to go to Eastern. My mom graduated from Eastern and my cousin Donald as well. My mom didn't think that would be a good decision so I opted to go to Phelps Career Senior High School to study Architectural Drafting.

Chapter III: High School and College Years | The Story of Eboni

During my high school selection process, I wanted to select a school that offered a trade program in addition to my regular high school classes. I choose Phelps because they had an architectural drafting program. I was introduced to drafting in the summer youth program I attended a summer ago.

After selecting a trade program, I would finally get a chance to participate in extra-curricular activities such as sports, student government, band, etc. My desire was to play sports, join the band and play saxophone and participate in student government.

My freshman year I played Junior Varsity basketball and baseball which I loved. I tried the band but it wasn't a good fit. My love for Go-Go music lead me to try participating in the band but it just didn't come together at that time so I joined the Student Government.

My junior year, Phelps started their football program which I was extremely excited about. I didn't get an opportunity to play in the neighborhood because I had to babysit my sister. With academics going well, my involvement with sports and other school activities, it gave me little time to miss my father which was still a major issue for me.

In addition to all the other challenges of being a teenager in high school, how you dressed ranked up there with your popularity. I was able to raise to the occasion in most not all areas other than the fashion department. I would often share with a few of my close friends and cousin my concerns and they would always try to help out. Since jonin' on people got me in trouble in Junior High, I didn't want to risk punishment again because I acted out. My cousin Reinard wore a lot of Ralph Lauren Polo. That probably started my obsession with the brand. So whenever I was in need fashion wear for events, parties, etc. he would come to the rescue and let me borrow something of his. That meant the world to me and I took extra special care of his clothing because of it. Little gestures like that also prevented me from turning to the streets to make the money myself. Even with my mother's warnings and understanding the risk of the game, some days it just got to be too much to bare. And on top of that, all the girls were into the guys that could dress well. Playing sports was cool; being best dressed was cooler.

During my junior year, I met my high school sweetheart Eboni. Eboni was probably my first "real" girlfriend. I had a few young ladies that I talked to on the phone like everyone did in that day but nothing official. In and around Phelps, you would have thought

Eboni and I were married. We were together all the time. When you saw me, you saw her and vice versa.

Eboni was also the first girl I was intimate with. My mother pulled me to the side as soon as she found out we were dating and had the "don't bring any babies into this world you can't take care of" speech. She didn't know if we were sexually active or not but she was just being proactive. Eboni and I spent a lot of weekends away from home at her sisters' apartment. Her sister was super cool and fun. She used to let us spend the night and watch her two kids while we were there. It was a chance for me to be away from home, be with my girl and of course doing something we weren't supposed to be doing, having sex.

We were safe for the most part but of course had our moment when we weren't so safe. There would be weekends when her sister and boyfriend would fill the fridge and make sure we had a couple dollars to move around if we wanted to in exchange for babysitting the girls. For the both of us, babysitting was enough of an introduction to parenthood for us to be safe and use protection more often than not.

My mother was very uncomfortable with this arrangement that went from once a month to almost every weekend. We would start to get into it about it which I'm sure was very frustrating for her trying to raise a boy to be a man without my dad's help especially given the fact that they had me so young. My mom was only 19 when she got pregnant with me. I'm sure a good measure of her if not all didn't want to see me repeat the same cycle. But when you're young, inexperienced and "in love", everything falls on deaf ears.

So with school, sports and my relationship going pretty well, I was in a really good space. I got news from my coaches that I was selected for the All-Star game my senior year. In that same year, I was selected as Homecoming King. Life couldn't get much better. I was looking at different colleges and trying to sort out what the next move would be after school. College was my first option but I did have an interest in the Armed Forces. For a lot of the men in my immediate family, they at some point in time serviced this country and it would have been a great honor to follow in that tradition. It wasn't until later in life that I found out my father was in the Marines.

Even with all the accomplishments and praise I received from others, nothing could take the place of me hearing from him that he was proud of me. I would always hear it from other people, always. My father was an all-around hustler. If there was a dollar to be made, he would find a way to make it. He spent a lot of time in the streets but never anything messy to my knowledge. He was just always about the dollar and making it. Every time I saw a family member or friend of the family they would say the same thing: "I saw your dad. He said he's proud of you and to keep up the good work". I had very mixed emotions about being what I call "blown off" by my own father. So I had a lot of soul searching to do to try to keep myself in check and avoid hating him for not being there for me.

I have other siblings that got some of his time and I just wanted my time. A lot of my motivation for doing well in everything was to impress him and to show him that I wasn't a mistake or I at least deserved some of his time.

After getting past these "moments" I would have thinking about my relationship with my father, I wanted to focus on myself and my senior year activities. So as for most kids in High School, Senior Prom was a pretty big deal. My mom did the best she could to assist with Prom but just didn't have enough make it happen alone. The Principal of Phelps at the time, "Bull" Johnson, and I were pretty close. He knew my family and always looked out when he could when I needed it. He was very instrumental in my decision to go to college after high school.

I let Mr. Johnson know that Prom would probably be too much for my mom to handle by herself financially. Mr. Johnson took me to get most of what I needed to enjoy my Prom night. That's a gesture I will never forget and that's one of the instances in my life that remind me to 'pay it forward'.

After talking over my college options with those close to me, I got accepted to and decided to attend Virginia Union University. It would be my first time leaving my mother and living away from DC. I was both afraid and anxious at the same time. This was a chance to establish myself and it gave me a new scenery and perceptive. Eboni had mixed emotions about my decision to leave home but she did support me. I graduated a year before her so she still had another year at Phelps while I moved to Richmond, VA to attend college.

With all the new challenges and expectations of college life, I still had to learn how to handle being on my own and dealing with a long distance relationship. Even as a young man, I wanted to remain faithful to my girlfriend. While most people were breaking up high school relationships, I wanted to keep mine going because I still cared for Eboni very much. In hindsight, I probably should have ended the relationship because of the distance and because we would way too young to take on something so serious. Along with that decision, I had to turn away advances from women and I have to refrain from pursuing women that I was very attracted to. That's a bit much to ask of an18 year old but it was the standard for me and I tried it anyway.

So here I am at Virginia Union, stressing about everything, broke and hungry always. I had side hustles and an overnight job at the Post Office but it wasn't enough to make ends meet most times.

Dwight was a cool guy from Rochester, NY that was trying to figure out what to do now that we're here just like me and my first roommate. My sport at the time I choose to pursue was basketball, his was football. Dwight and I formed a brotherly bond that last to this day. We were there for one another and leaned on one another for everything. Honestly he was the closed thing I had to a blood brother.

During a school break near Eboni's Senior Prom, I was having second thoughts about continuing our relationship. The distance and stresses of school and life began to take its toll on me. With money already being thin and wanting out of the relationship, I told Eboni that I didn't want to attend her Prom. For as bad as that sounds, I knew that I wouldn't be very good company on what's supposed to be a night of celebration for her. I was happy for her, just didn't want to be with her. After continually refusing to go, her big sister called and asked me to go with her and I said that I would for her.

Just as I predicted, the night was a disaster. I didn't look like I wanted to be there and nor did I act like I wanted to be there. At the end of the evening, I asked to be dropped off at my house and they drove off. I felt horrible but I felt like I did what was best for me at the time. I probably could have handled it a lot better but I did the best I could with the experience I had. I never really had to break-up with a girl nor break her heart so like most other people in my life starting with my father, I just left.

After the break up with Eboni, I headed back to Virginia Union to try out for the basketball team and stir up some interest in staying at school. I didn't like struggling as much as I did but I didn't want to go back home. For some reason, moving back to DC meant failure. The basketball team held a few open call tryouts for basketball walk-ons that could potentially make the team. I got injured during the tryouts and passed on that opportunity.

No longer interested in being a college student and refusing to move back to DC, I decided to visit my Cousin Donald who was stationed a few hours away. He would come down every now and then to pick me up to visit the Army base where he was stationed and his home. Even from his high school days, I was always impressed with my cousin Donald and his life. I watched him as he came up through the ranks, buy a home and drive nice cars. So I said to myself, if the Army is good enough for him, it would be good enough for me. In June of 1993, I decided to join the United States Army.

Chapter IV: Joining the Army | The Story of Tiffany

In June of 1993, I enlisted in the U.S. Army. Feeling excited, scared, regretful and missing home is a lot to try to process when you're being yelled at by a drill instructor for several weeks. However I received plenty of boot camp training before I even enlisted in the Army. My mother was great but she didn't play any games when it came to certain things. She was pretty strict when it came to keeping the house clean and everything in the house having a place or position. Those lessons have stuck with me to this day. And, before finding the Lord, she could yell and curse with the best of them.

Boot camp was an interesting mix of time management, thinking under pressure and adapting to situations and implementing resolutions so that was easy for me. While you're doing your initial entry into the military, you select your job assignment. I chose logistics/supply for my occupation.

After leaving boot camp in Ft. Sill, OK, I moved onto Ft. Lee, VA to complete my job training. I met a few impressive soldiers. One of those soldiers was my main drill instructor. He was very knowledgeable, decorated but more importantly, he was well respected. During the decision making process for my permanent duty station, he was instrumental in giving all the information necessary to be successful and fast track my way to the next rank and pay grade.

In addition to selecting Ft. Bragg, NC as my permanent duty station, I decided to sign up to become a paratrooper with the 82nd Airborne Division.

While stationed at Ft. Lee, I meet a young lady named Tiffany. Tiffany is also in the Army and in the same class as me. She's also the first woman I had taken serious since I left Eboni. Tiffany and I dated for about 4 months and things were going well. Only major issue was that she was headed to a different duty station after our job training was over.

Near the end of our job training, she invited me to her hometown of Kentucky. I went to Kentucky one way and left with a totally different perspective. Once I got to Kentucky, she told me that she was pregnant. I asked how far along, she said a few weeks. I was shocked but I wasn't because I remember times when I used protection and when I didn't.

So fully ready to take on my responsibilities, I asked her to marry me. The look on her face told me my answer, and then I heard it. The answer was no. I was surprised by her response nor did I understand it. In addition to her "no" to my marriage proposal, she informed me that she would be having an abortion as well, and because I don't believe in abortion, I was double hurt.

I was hurt for many reasons. The "no" to the proposal, the decision to have an abortion that she made on her own and most importantly my opinion on the matter having no place. I had no voice. I had to accept whatever her decision was because it's her body. It was my first hard lesson in understanding how as a man I don't have a voice once a woman gets pregnant and I felt powerless.

Once I left Kentucky, our relationship was never the same. For the most part we parted ways and wished one another well.

Chapter V: Fort Bragg, North Carolina

Once job training was over, I headed back to DC for a few weeks before I had to report to my permanent duty station at Ft. Bragg. While I'm at home I ran into Eboni. We went out a few times to see if we could rekindle what we once had but to no avail. We were two different people and for the most part had grown apart.

That next month I had to report to Ft. Bragg, NC which was my permanent duty station for the next four years. Once I arrived, I was in a hold over unit until they found a unit for me to be assigned to. While I was in hold over, drill instructors asked who wanted to volunteer for jump school. As I raised my hand to volunteer, a young lady raised her hand, Victoria. There weren't that many guys that raised their hands so that made her stand out.

Victoria and I end up going to the same hold over unit before we headed jump school in Ft. Benning, GA. We started dating while we were in the hold over unit and it carried over to jump school. By the time we got back to Ft. Bragg from jump school, we were engaged.

For the first time ever, it felt right. When I proposed to Tiffany, it was because she was pregnant. Not really a fix for the situation but I would have made the sacrifice for my child to have the proper family structure.

Chapter VI: The Story of Victoria

Once we get back from jump school, I proposed to Victoria. One of the few differences we had in the beginning was a major one, religion. My religious practice, Christianity and hers was Islam. I had always taken an interest in Islam so I did some research and decided to convert to Islam. There was a lot of new information to take in and understand in such a short period of time.

I converted during our first visit to Minnesota. After meeting her parent and a long conversation, I converted to Islam. I was good with my decision and I had to live with that decision and my decision to marry Victoria. We drive back from Minnesota to NC and begin to settle into our lives together as husband and wife.

We get back to Ft. Bragg and married life begins. We move into our first apartment, we're buying furniture, bought our first vehicle. You know, married folk stuff. I get my assignment to an Aviation unit as a Supply Clerk and she's assigned to another unit doing personnel work. Both of us are on jump status which means we have scheduled jumps during our tour at Ft. Bragg. I'm still excited about jumping because there was a different recognition that came with being an Airborne Paratrooper. First thing you notice was the burgundy beret. The second thing that stands out is jump boots. In addition to the pride you carry as a soldier, there was additional pay for jumping from airplanes, $110 if I'm not mistaken. Not a lot of money today but to a private in the Army, that was an exceptional pay increase.

Before we got married, one of the things we talked about was having children. The both of us wanted a large family. She comes from a large family and I'd always wanted a big family of my own. One day we're having a discussion about having children and when to start a family. My argument was logical and direct. Let's continue to enjoy one another, build our bank account in preparation for such an event. She was ready to start now, right now.

A few weeks pass and I'm noticing that I'm eating a lot more, sleeping more, really sluggish at work and just over all. I suggested to her that she might be pregnant and she denied it. A few weeks after that she told me she was pregnant. I just looked at her with such disappointment. This told me a few things. The first thing it told me is that my body doesn't lie. I don't know what other men experience when they get a woman pregnant, but I know I feel some of those symptoms. Second thing it told me was, she was on the pill and stopped taking the pill to get pregnant which was totally against what we had discussed not even a month before.

I was disappointed but I knew I had to get past it. I was going to be a father. Other issues start to arise which didn't make the situation any more comfortable. Through discussion I find out that she no longer wants to be in the Army and is planning to go back home. But that information didn't come directly from her so I took it with a grain of salt. Communication with her is starting to break down, she's closing herself off and it's taking a toll on our marriage.

Victoria had an upcoming trip to Minnesota which she was very excited about. I was excited for her because that seemed to be the only thing that she would talk or smile about. I gave her as much space as she needed for the sake of the marriage and health of the baby. I didn't want to bring any more stress than was already there. The space I gave her also gave me a chance to have some space and think. I would often have dreams and visions of what our baby would look like. It was a little scary for me mainly because I had no one to really talk to or share things with.

I was really into sports as an outlet once I joined the Army. Both of us played basketball and flag football for our units. There was a guy

Victoria worked with, Jones, which was into sports as well and was an all-around cool dude.

Jones was married as well so we would often exchange war stories as two young married military men.

Victoria leaves for her trip to Minnesota so that gave me plenty of free time. I hung out with Jones and his wife often. One day Jones has a cookout at his house and we all plan to go to the club in the city later that evening. Good company, good food, good times. Later that evening, Jones and his wife get into a heated argument as he would often tell me they would. I did my best to look away, stay out of the way and mind my business. I know how hard it was maintaining my own marriage so I wanted no parts of what was wrong with theirs. Until… Victoria's name comes up. With this very strange look on my face I say to the both of them: "Excuse me??? What does MY wife have to do with this???" Jones' wife looked at me, he looked at her and she proceeded to tell everything.

According to her, Victoria and Jones had been carrying on this "affair" of sorts. She has been drinking and was super emotional so she yelled about a lot of stuff. The only stuff I cared about were the things being said about his interaction with my wife. According to her, there were some letters being written back and forth and some meet-ups that took place between the two of them. So this otherwise normal cookout just turned into the set of The Maury Show.

After yelling and screaming at Jones she just finally got fed up and ran into the kitchen and grabbed a knife, a big one. She was going to hurt him bad. For as much as I wanted to hurt him too, my protective instincts kicked in to hold her back. Mad that she went and got a knife, Jones runs upstairs to his bedroom to get a gun, a .22 if I'm not mistaken. So here I am between two people full of anger, both with weapons and I'm trying to play peacemaker.

One of the other females at the party grabbed his wife and I grabbed Jones and took him outside. We both got in my car and left. The last thing I wanted was for the military police to show up with all this activity and someone go to jail. I drove Jones on the other side of the base and parked. We talked extensively about all that had happened over the past few hours. I demanded that he give me the letters that had been saved so that I could confront my wife. With hesitance, once we got back to the house he gave me the letters he had saved.

At this point, all types of thoughts are running through my mind. How long had this been going on? Is this why she's been so distant? Is she even carrying my baby? I hadn't touched a drink in while I was in the military, but that night, I drank a lot. I cried a lot, I got angry; I broke a lot of stuff in our apartment. The next day I waited until I thought she was up and I made the called to my wife in Minnesota with the letters she wrote to Jones in hand.

Our conversation started off normal. Questions about her, how she's feeling, the baby, the family… Then I got right to it. I asked her what was going on between her and Jones and how long. She said she didn't know what I was talking about. I started reading the letters, one after another. She was silent. She had nothing to say. She tried to explain her position but I wasn't hearing it. Once I stopped yelling, she confessed to everything, apologized and we got off the phone. That would be the last time I talked to her while she was on her trip.

Victoria got back in town a couple days after that phone call. When I picked her up from the airport I could tell that something was off. I didn't expect for it to be a celebration once she got back home but I handled things the best way I could at the time. About a week passes and as we are driving home she turns to me and says: "My dad will be down in a few weeks with a U-Haul to get me and my stuff. I'm moving back to Minnesota." I was devastated. All I could wonder was why? Why are you leaving now? I'm about to be a father and you're leaving.

Even with all that had gone down between us, I didn't want to lose my family. For about a week, I asked her to stay, she said no every time and I wasn't going to beg. If ever you have to beg for a thing no matter what it is, you've lost all respect for yourself. So I have to respect her decision to leave.

About a month passed, and sure as my name is what it is, her dad drove from Minnesota to North Carolina to get his daughter/my wife and child. He packed up her stuff, looked me in my eyes, said a few words and pulled off. That would be the last time I saw my wife until she gave birth to our daughter.

Chapter VII: Alicia Revisited

After dealing with Victoria and that situation, I wanted to go home and regroup. I need to take some time to myself to sort things out, to see how I felt, my next move, etc. I was nearing the end of my active duty obligation to the Army and deciding whether I wanted to leave the military or stay. Because there were so many things that went wrong and negative energy tied to that experience, I decided to leave the Army after my 4 year commitment.

While I was home in DC visiting, I crossed paths with a mutual friend that knew Alicia. We exchange information and I call Alicia. Now if you remember this was my Junior High School first crush, so I was still a little nervous even with us being older. We went out to dinner later that week and had a great time. We were able to catch up, talk about old times, etc. There was a chemistry there that wasn't there when we were teenagers. She was grown and I was grown and we made it happen.

Shortly after that we were talking and she got accepted to a school in NC. I'm thinking to myself the stars are lining up in my favor right now. As I'm about to file for divorce from Victoria, Alicia comes along ready and waiting. I probably wasn't ready or totally healed from the last situation but I wasn't going to let me being hurt by someone else interrupt my happiness with the next person.

I contacted Victoria one last time to see if she was interested in moving here to see if we could make it work but to no avail. She didn't want to leave her hometown. So with that being said, I filed for divorce so that we both could move on with our lives. No point in staying together miserable if no one is willing to sacrifice living arrangements in addition to the love being diminished from the trust that was destroyed before.

A few weeks later I assisted Alicia with her move to NC. We continued to see one another for the next few months. So I'm driving back and forth pretty often because I'm really into her and being with her is better than I thought it would be. I was on cloud nine.

About a month passes with her being in NC and I start to notice changes. The calls are a little less often, the visits are starting to slow down. One weekend I drive up to her dorm. She sits me down and tells me she doesn't want anything more than friendship. I was crushed. I thought we were working towards something and she just wants to be friends now. So I ended up leaving and just cutting my losses. I was really hoping that it worked out because we had such great chemistry. But what's meant to be shall be and if it's not then it won't be. That's life.

I didn't have much time to waste on trying to revive that situation so I shifted my time, energy and efforts to going to visit my daughter for the first time. I saved my next 3 or 4 paychecks and drove to Minnesota to see my baby girl for the first time. She was as beautiful as I envisioned her. I had a great trip to Minnesota. Nothing sparked when I went as I thought it might. I had to accept that I was going to have to love my baby girl from a far.

Chapter VIII: The Story of Dawn

About a year passed and I moved back home to DC. It's time for me to develop a plan and put that plan in motion. For me, that meant leaving love alone for a minute and giving my career the attention it deserved. After all, I did have a daughter to provide for. I was on the job hunt for months. Because I knew I was leaving the military, I should have actually started my job/career search about a year in advance of me exiting the service. Lesson Learned.

Since I was back home with no real job prospect lined up, I had to move back in with my Mom and sister. When I left for college after high school my mom had condensed the size of their living quarters which is totally understandable. The less people that are around the less space you need. So I really appreciated her allowing me to come back home. I didn't want to be there long so I knew what I had to do. Find a job and a place to stay fast.

To relieve stress while I was at Ft. Bragg, I found roller skating to be an outlet. Roller skating combined my two favorite things: Music and physical activity. I was also looking to return to my Christian roots as well. Islam wasn't a fit for me spiritually but I certainly respect those who commit to and practice it.

I was on this spiritual quest of some sort. I was reading the bible a lot more than usual, listening to more gospel music. Nothing against secular music at all, I just needed something that would fill me with substance rather than make me dance.

During my spiritual quest, I started to attend more gospel skate sessions. These sessions were held on Friday nights versus my usual

Thursday or Sunday night sessions. While at one of the Gospel night sessions, I met a beautiful older woman, Dawn. And when I say older, at the time I was only 24 years old. She was 13 years my elder but she had the youthful appearance of someone my age. She had the most amazing eyes and a beautiful smile.

Dawn was a Christian with a very strong spiritual foundation which I was very drawn to. I introduced myself and we exchanged phone numbers. From that moment on, we talked all the time. We had such a strong chemistry but it was more than physical. I connected with her in a way I had never connected with another woman and that was spiritually which at the time was exactly what I needed.

A few months pass and I have a trip set to go visit my daughter who is now living in Texas with her mother and new man. When I get to Texas, we all have a conversation to put everything on the table. My expectation is that you don't let anything happen to my daughter. We agreed and shook hands like men. I respected his position and he respected mine.

While in Texas, I talked to Dawn every day. The time that we were apart was extremely tough. It felt like I was missing a part of me and she was missing a part of her. So right after I get back to DC, we get married. During our courtship, there was no intimacy at all. We barely even kissed as to not entice one another. So needless to say right after we got married, she got pregnant with our son.

I wasn't really in the position to become a father again primarily due to the obligations I have to my daughter in Texas and that I wasn't employed. I prayed, we prayed a lot that I would find employment. But we had no business having a baby without both incomes in place. That's like purchasing a vehicle and then trying to figure out how you're going to pay for the car note, insurance, maintenance, etc. Life doesn't work that way. If the money isn't right, there's no way we should have had a baby. That was a hard lesson learned.

With that said, I was on the hunt for a job heavy. I took any job that came along at the time. I did everything from deliveries to day labor and couldn't find a stable job and I got frustrated a lot. I felt less than a man because she was doing all the providing. She was taking care of the house, her 13 year old daughter, me and whoever else she could help out. That's just the type of giving spirit she had.

She would often tell me to be patient and that things would work out in God's time. When you're young and you need money, that's the last thing you really want to hear even though it's the first thing you need to hear. My frustration, insecurities and immaturity began to take its toll on our relationship. In addition, her daughter and I started to get into it about various issues. I was in a tough spot to discipline her when I was essentially in the same position as her. Our relationship turned from a husband/wife relationship to a mother/son relationship almost overnight.

It was a bad space for all parties involved. She was pregnant with our son and I didn't want to be the further cause of any stress of any sort. And since we could not get along, I'd just rather be gone. My great grandmother passed on an old saying that says: "If I can't do you any good, I certainly won't do you any harm." So rather than continue to be a burden to the situation, I did what was best and I left.

I felt terrible that I was breaking up another family, horrible actually. I was even more disappointed because I helped bring another child into this world that I'm having trouble providing for. And, I was leaving my son which brought up emotions about me and my father. For as much as I was angry and disappointed in him for not being there for me, I was starting to see through my own life's journey that things aren't always what they seem.

Toward the end of my marriage to Dawn, I moved back in with my mother and sister. I was really close with the first family of the church that Dawn and I attended. I was cool with the pastors' kids which were around the same age. I was invited to a function, a birthday party if I'm not mistaken, and I was introduced to their Cousin, Jasmine.

Chapter IX: The Story of Jasmine

Upon meeting Jasmine I'll have to admit that it was probably love at first site. Everyone has a type, we all do. Without effort upon meeting her, she hit everything on my checklist visually. She was also smart, funny and she was a good friend in my time of need. I had just loss my dad and just needed someone to be there. There were still tons of unresolved issues there but there was nothing I could really do about it with him being gone. At his funeral I cried like he was there every day, at every game cheering me on. Deep down inside was a lot of anger and resentment for not being there.

Shortly after moving back in with my mother, Jasmine and I started dating. I was in between job and looking which was still a bit frustrating. My relationship with Dawn had soured because of my decision to leave and dating someone that went to the same church didn't help things. My mother was a bit fed up with the moving back and forth which was understandable. She sat me down one day and expressed her view on things and since I was living in her dwelling she was entitled to that. After that conversation, I was given 30 days to find a job and a place to stay. I sat there in shock for a sec. I'm sitting there thinking the one person that's supposed to always be there for me is kicking me out. But it was quite the contrary.

My mother was very calculated when she did things or said things. Everything was said or done with a purpose. Sometimes she would give you the purpose, other times you would have to figure it out. I learned a lot of lessons this way. It forced me to think even when I didn't want to. So with her deadline of 30 days, I wiped my tears and hit the ground running. I found my first job in Information Technology (IT) flipping through the yellow pages and calling random employers and I was approved for an apartment in 22 days. I was super excited and when I told her the great news, she just smiled and said "I've been praying for you" and went on about her way.

I knew exactly what that smile meant. It meant I'm proud of you, keep up the good work. She didn't have to say it, her smile said it all. That taught me a very valuable parenting lessons as well. We can't always be there and baby our kids. We can't always make things easy for them. We can help but they have to learn how to fly on their own. Give them as much information as they need to get the mission accomplished, pray and move out of the way and let God do the rest. There's no tell how long I would have stayed at her house just out of being comfortable. She removed my comfort zone and I had to adapt.

In the meantime, things were going ok between Jasmine and I but there were issues detected early in. Because my ex-wife went to the same church, there was friction. She didn't care much for Dawn and later came to find out she didn't care much for my son either. I tried to understand the situation from her point of view and be fair to her feelings about it but it was a struggle.

In the midst of my relationship dilemma, I decided that my career path would continue in Information Technology (IT). My very first

IT job like most others that start out was a help desk position. I enjoyed the technology part of the job and learning new things but what I liked more was helping people understand things that they once hadn't about computers and technology. IT was a very rewarding career and it paid very well if you choose the right discipline and found the right opportunity.

While making my way through relationship and career, I met Ron West at church. Ron was the big brother I never had growing up. Come to find out we grew up blocks away from each other and never crossed paths when we were coming up. He was more experienced in life, marriage, spiritually which is why I learned so much from him. When I wasn't thinking straight, he was the one person that could bring me back around or make me see things from a different perspective.

He was very instrumental in keeping me on track with Jasmine. There were many days I wanted to throw in the towel because of something she did or said. He taught me to be a man of understanding, patience, love and forgiveness. That was a huge lesson coming from another man. I've always had strong female inspirations and he was one of the first males to teach me on that level.

Jasmine and I dated for about a year and a half. This was an ion compared to my other engagements and marriages. I was happy that I finally took the time to get to know her better and give myself a chance to see all sides of her. So with my relationship, not perfect, but going ok and my career moving along, I proposed to Jasmine. She said yes.

After getting engaged, I got really focused on my career and wanted to make myself more marketable and valuable as an employee. With that thought in mind, I decide to attend ITT Technical Institute for undergraduate studies. This would also keep me busy and out of any kind of trouble.

Jasmine had times when she could be selfish. I would sometimes chalk it up to her being an only child and there were other times that I thought if you know better you should do better. I don't mind my woman being a little spoiled, not at all. As a matter of fact, I love to spoil my woman. But she has to have enough balance within herself to bring it all back to reality.

A few months after our engagement, we started marriage counselling with one of the elder couples of the church. They had been married 30 plus years and they were always a great example to me so I was excited to be in the midst of this wisdom. Outside of my conversations with Jasmine, they couple detected some issues between Jasmine and I. The wife looked right at Jasmine and said: "If you make him choose between you and his son, you're going to lose your husband". Clearly that bit of information fell on deaf ears because she didn't make any real adjustments to her behavior.

We would go from having issues every other weekend when I had my son, to her having issues with my son being in the wedding, to me calling the wedding off. Whenever I got to that point, she would show flashes of what could be. Once there was some consistent behavior, I decided to marry her. I prayed and I fasted heavy for weeks to hopefully guard against any further issues. What I've come to learn is, all the prayer in the world doesn't change people. People have to want to change. It's that simple.

Regardless of what people think, the universe has a way of giving you back what you put out. If you put good energy out, good energy returns, same with bad energy. With that said, bad things started to happen. First, the wedding pictures got ruined. Something happened with them being exposed too soon and all but a handful of the pictures were ruined.

She was unfortunately in a bad car accident which had a tremendous effect on our relationship as a whole. She couldn't work so that meant I had to carry the load financially. It affected our ability to be intimate which was one of the things that kept us together. And it was just one thing after another.

I tried my best to manage and salvage things with Jasmine but I didn't feel like she wanted me. I felt like she was tired of being single. She wanted a husband to say she had a husband. I was a husband and a father which was probably more than she wanted to really deal with.

Once she filed her lawsuit for the accident which left her out of work and in lots of pain, I was already distancing myself emotionally. I was hurt and disappointed and I felt like she used me for status purposes. After about two years of back and forth with Jasmine, I decided that it was best for me to be on my way. I moved out a few months after our last talk and we divorced later that year.

Chapter X: The Story of Leslie

Leslie and I met during the decline of my marriage to Jasmine. She was really cool and a great relief from the confusion of my life at home. We met during one of the skate sessions in Maryland. For me, roller skating and the music of DJ Stormin' Norman was my weekly release. It was a place of refuge for me and a lot of the other skaters I knew. It was the one place they could go and just be free for a couple hours.

Upon meeting Leslie, I didn't tell her I was married. It was honestly about the flirt for me. She was very pretty, funny and I enjoyed spending time with her but I knew it wasn't going any further than that. But of course the more time and laughs you share with a person, things start to grow.

I called Leslie one day and asked her to meet me. I told her upon meeting her that I was married and we needed to put a hold on what was starting between us until I was officially divorced. I still liked her of course but I didn't want it to be a situation where I was leaving Jasmine for Leslie. I had been down that road so I wanted to avoid it.

Against my better judgment, we continued on with our friendship until it developed into a relationship. I tell Leslie my backstory and she told me hers. She had never been married. She was very accomplished in her life and career. For her, the one thing she didn't have that she treasured was motherhood. She'd wanted to have a baby for some time now but it just hadn't panned out. She was interested in marriage but it wasn't at the top of her list. I wasn't really interested in marrying again but I did want to have another child. And since I didn't have a child with Jasmine, we talked about having a child and raising it together.

Once my marriage was finalized from Jasmine, I made the hasty mistake of moving in with Leslie. Another road I had been down but Leslie appeared to be different. When I first moved in, it was pretty cool. We enjoyed one another, traveled, etc. We had time to enjoy us. In addition, both work and school were coming along well.

After about a year of just us, she was ready to have a baby. I shared my views on the matter. I wanted to finish undergrad at least and get another job making more money. So I'm at this crossroad again… She's ready to have a baby and I'm not. So me being who I am, I give in and say let's do it. My main issue with getting pregnant so soon was that our foundation as a couple wasn't strong either. What can happen sometimes is that the baby becomes the focus of everything and the two people that came together can drift apart. It happens all the time. It's happened in my past. The relationship then becomes all about taking care of and providing for this new life that's been brought into the world. A lot of couples experience trouble in their relationship and or marriage because they have yet made a full investment in one another. This is what I believe happened to myself and Leslie.

Shortly after that decision, she gets pregnant. She is happy and satisfied and I'm happy but empty because had to sacrifice what made sense for what she wanted. I was tired. Tired of giving in, tired of fulfilling the desires of others and having to figure out the rest. I snapped… and lost it.

March 6, 2012… I experienced what's called a stress induced manic episode. I drove my 2001 Nissan Maxima 120mph into on-coming traffic, hit five cars along the way. The car flipped out of control 10 or 15 times then rolled to a complete stop. Medical staff arrived on the scene just in time to pull me out of the car. After I was pulled from the car, it burst into flames.

I was rushed to Washington Hospital Center where I was diagnosed with and treated for Bipolar Disorder I. After leaving the triage area, I was sent straight to the psychiatric ward. I was dead center of the scariest time of my life. All I could remember thinking was I pray that I didn't hurt or kill anyone because of my actions. After receiving the police report, no one was hurt or died in the accident.

I was at Washington Hospital Center for about 7 days trying to fix the right mixture of medication to treat Bipolar Disorder I. The medications and effects vary from person to person so it makes finding the right medications extremely hard especially on the person being treated.

I was in and out of the hospital for months trying to get "stable" and figure out my next move. It was suggested that I move back in with my mother for a brief time and then moved back in with Leslie. Because I was still trying to sort out things with and for myself and she was doing her best to raise our daughter. And because I'm never one to force an issue, I moved back into my apartment at Mayfair. After several arguments, we agreed to part way and co-parent as best we could.

Chapter XI: Time of Recovery

After things finally ended with Leslie, I went into this cycle of going in and out of the hospital to get treatment for my condition. I was still very much in shock from everything that had happened the past year from the accident, to my diagnosis, to losing my relationship with Leslie and feeling like I destroyed yet another family and left my daughter behind.

I battled with depression more than I did mania after the accident so I was back and forth to the hospital trying to figure out how to live with this illness. I think I went through just about every medication you can prescribe for Bipolar Disorder in addition to the outpatient program which conducts the talk therapy part of your recovery plan.

I went through several stages where I was just flat out embarrassed behind it all. I lost friends, a few family members and relationships all behind something I couldn't control. While on the path to recovery, I still had to look for and find a job. One thing about life, it stops for no one. This is the reason you have to cherish each day as if it's your last.

My big brother Ron West was one of the few important people in my life at the time that helps me on my road to becoming whole again. He would always call, come by, and pick me up just to get out of the house. He kept my spirits high and that was exactly what I needed.

After months of being unemployed, I found a job the week of my birthday in 2012. The timing could not have been better. I was able to finish my undergraduate studies at ITT Technical Institute and moved onto a Master's Degree Program at Strayer University.

Shortly after all started to fall back into place for me, I lose my best friend in the world. Ron West passed away from this life April 28, 2012. It was first time I really cried since I loss my father 9 years before. I was hurt but he taught me to be strong. I thought and still think on the times we shared, the laugh, the tears, the prayers. It was an honor to have known such a special guy. He helped me to remember to never take things for granted and to always stay humble. Two lessons I will never forget.

Chapter XII: The Story of Denise

After my relationships with Dawn and Leslie, I vowed never to date anyone from the skating rink again. Why? Because my track record with that isn't too good and again that's my place of refuge and if we break up, I'd still have to see that person. I've seen that movie play out way too many times with my other skate friends.

So of course right after I make this vow, I found interest in another young woman that was a regular at the rink. She was a handful from the start but I should have known better. She was different, feisty, unfiltered. I didn't always like her unpredictable emotions but I could always respect her honesty.

We had a few things in common. Both of us had 3 kids and had been through a few things and really wanted to just chill and have a good time. We had good chemistry but that attitude would get the best of her a lot. She shared some of her past which gave me a point of reference for why she acted out the way she did sometimes. But my policy is and will always be, if you know better do better.

We spent a lot of time together early in the relationship which was probably part of the reason we didn't work in the end. I'm sure it was. I was coming from a space where it was just me and I had a lot of free time. So to go from that to basically having a live in girlfriend and family was too much too soon.

She was living between my place and her sister's place trying to get herself together. She worked off and on, which was also a pretty big turn off, but you try not to judge people where they are but where they're going.

That temper though. That for me was a major issue. We broke up behind something she did and she keyed both sides of my vehicle. I had never experienced anything like that in my life.

I went to the police and filed a report to have my vehicle fixed and took out a stay away order against her. When she showed up to court, the order was granted and that was that.

A few weeks pass and we see each other in passing. I reach out to pretty much settle everything so that we can remain civil about things and we ended up getting back together. We decided to give the relationship another try. We agreed that both of us could have handled the previous situation a lot better.

About a month passes and she's having a tough time finding a job in DC. She comes up with a plan to move to Florida with a female friend of hers. I don't want her to go but she had her mind set on going. I'm not one to stand in anyone's way if their mind is made up so I wished her the best.

She moves to Florida to set up and get life going there. We're still a couple at this point so she's back and forth to DC to see me and visit family. Not even a few weeks after she moved there and couldn't find a job and she got into a disagreement with her female friend, she moved back to DC. All of this happened within about a two month span of time.

Now we're back to the same arrangement of her living between my house and her sister's house. Fed up with all the sporadic behavior, I decide it's best for her to go ahead and get her life in order and for me to move on.

After arguing on the phone about the entire ordeal, I tell her to come to my apartment to get all of her belongings and to return the key to my apartment. She came and got her belongings, I got my keys and it was over. Moral of this story is: When someone shows you who they are, believe them.

So in preparation, I packed all of her belongings up neatly and sat them on the couch in the living room. I took a picture of the belongings and video on a camera for evidence just in case anything came up. The damage to my car after the first breakup was more than enough drama for me.

The apartment I lived in was located on the third floor of the building and I could see the traffic on the street from my kitchen window. I saw her as she pulled into the parking lot and storming up the stairs. When she got my floor, I had the door open so that she could just get her stuff and go. I asked her to get her belongings, leave my key on the table and go. There was no need for her to go any further that the living room but she insisted on searching the apartment for more things.

As she's gathering her things, she's calling me every fouls name under the sun. I'm standing there holding the door and waiting for her to finish so that I can proceed with the rest of my night. She stopped a few times to get in my face to yell, point her finger… Trying to provoke me to respond to her and her foolishness. Once she was done, I slammed my door. In addition, she was being very loud and disruptive in the hallway which was disturbing my neighbors. I asked her to refrain from all the noise which only made her act out more.

Fed up with her antics, I told her I was calling the police. I didn't call the police; it was something I said to get her to calm down.

Ironically enough, as she was taking her things down to her car, a police car was pulling over a driver for a traffic stop in front of my building. I could see the police car from my window. She stopped dead in her track, ran over to the police to say something to the police officer. I could only imagine what kind of story she made up to tell the police officer. She was an extremely angry and spiteful person so I anticipated the worst.

I could hear the police officers making their way up the stairs to my apartment. Part of me was terrified because I had no idea what this woman said to them. The other part of me was ok because I know I had done no wrong. When they get to my floor, I was standing with the door open and I asked "may I help you gentleman?" One of the officers proceeded to say she reported a "domestic disturbance" in my apartment. I told both officers there was no "domestic disturbance". She is an ex-girlfriend that was asked to come to get her belongings and leave my premises. I asked that she get her things and leave my keys. Nothing more, nothing less.

The other officer turned to me and said she reported an assault. She said I pushed and shoved her and threw her things in the hallway.

The look I gave him probably got me arrested more than the incident. I looked him dead in the eyes and said to him: "Clearly this is a case where she's pissed off because I'm breaking up with her and she's an idiot. Look at me... I'm a pretty big guy, about 260 to be exact. Look at her... Do you see any evidence of assault? Do you see any marks, cuts, bruises?" I'll go with "no" because I didn't touch her. I didn't assault her. The officer proceeded to explain to me that if you curse at someone, that's verbal assault. I said to him "I didn't curse at her either. I held the door as she got her things and left." She also stated that I threw her things in the hallway so I proceeded to show the police officers the pictures and video with date and time stamps to prove that I was telling the truth. All that for naught.

The two officers stepped outside to talk to her and came back in. I knew that was a bad sign. One of the officers stepped back into my apartment. He proceeded to ask me to take off my jewelry and take out my shoes laces. With a puzzled look on my face I ask him: "Why would I do that?" He explained to me that I was under arrest for simple assault. I did as the officer asked. For the first time in my life,

I was in handcuffs and going to jail. To add insult to injury, she took out a "stay away" order on me, the exact same thing I did to her after our first break up. All I could think of at this point was the clearance process I was going through for my job and how I really didn't need any of this.

When I showed for court, the first person I saw was her mom. She apologized for her daughter actions. I told her thank you for the apology but she's a grown woman and she should be accountable for her own issues. Her brother called me and asked if I needed him to testify against her. I laughed and told him no thank you and that I would be ok. Real people know recognize real people so I had nothing further to say or prove. People know me and my character and they know hers.

I can honestly say I wasn't completely mad at her and her actions. I already knew the ignorance she was capable of. This was just the result of that ignorance. I tried to make it work again with someone that wasn't worth it the first time. We should never put ourselves back into situations we know aren't healthy for us. So instead of staying upset about the situation, I learned a valuable lesson and I'm a better person for it. Moral of the chapter, when someone shows

you who they are believe them.

Chapter XIII: The Story of Morgan

After the madness I experienced with Denise, I just needed a break from dating, understanding, forgiving, expectations, and all the things that come with being in a relationship. With school and my relationship with my kids on the front burner, I was in a good space. I was learning for the first time really how to live and be alone. I learned that being alone isn't all bad and I got a lot more done when I didn't have to worry about another person's thoughts, time or feelings.

One day on a store run, I ran into Morgan. Morgan and I had history and been between marriages in my 20's. We exchange information that day and met for drinks later that week. Shortly after that meeting we start dating and things went well early. She had two daughters. The oldest daughter I remember when she was younger and her youngest daughter I was getting to know. We had a cool little connection going. No pressure, just enjoying one another's company.

Once the weather broke for Spring, she invited me to a wine festival. I had never been to a wine festival so I was excited to go. And for the first time in a long time a woman was bringing me something I hadn't experienced. I'm not much of a drinker but I know and understand the basics of drinking. If you're going to drink, put something on your stomach to prevent the alcohol from consuming you or making you drunk.

She decided to get 3-4 bottles of wine but put very little on her stomach. Add the heat of the day, about 90 degrees, and you have a recipe for disaster. Needless to say the rest of the event was downhill from there.

I had to help her to the car where she almost threw up on the floor. She was able to pull herself together enough prevent that. Once we got back to my apartment, she was sleeping in the car and didn't get up for about 3 hours. I had to leave the car running and the air conditioning on so that she would be cool at least. Once she woke up from sleeping in the car, she came upstairs and slept another 8 hours.

I was thoroughly frustrated and embarrassed by her actions and ready to be done with being in a relationship with her. In addition to issues like that, her relationship with her oldest daughter was very turbulent. They would always argue, fussing almost fighting about everything. It used to trip me out how I would have to referee and be the voice of reason. It was just an environment that I wasn't used to.

A few months pass and things are ok for the most part. My best friend invites us out to his birthday bash at one of the local clubs in DC. When we get there I do the gentlemanly thing and offer her something to drink. I was still a bit sore from the previous incident involving alcohol but I didn't want to hold any grudges.

After she has her drink, that's when the fun started. I went to the bathroom to come back to the VIP area where she's bumping and grinding on my best friend. He's turned around dancing with another woman with this look on his face that said: "What's going on with your girl??!?!?!" I was pissed off, totally pissed off. For the second time, she had embarrassed me publicly. I was done, totally done.

I politely grabbed my jacket and headed to the exit. I didn't even say goodbye to anyone, I just left. She saw me leaving, grabbed her jacket and ran out behind me. I walked to my truck and popped the hatch. I took her bag out of seat of the truck, set it down on the sidewalk and asked her to find another way home. I was that mad.

She was begging, pleading: "What's wrong??? I didn't do anything???" The more she said it the madder I got. I got in my truck, started it up and pulled off. It was about 10 feet to the corner. As I turned the corner, something told me to stop. I thought to myself: "Even though you're pissed off at her, you have two daughters you wouldn't want anybody to leave stranded". It took everything in me but I told her to get in and I was taking her home. The rules were that she was not to talk to me. Just get in, once we got to her house, she would get out and be on her way.

As I'm driving to her house, I should have gotten pulled over and arrested. I was driving so fast to her house to get her away from me. Even though we went over the rule for transporting her to her residence, she still did what she wanted. She was crying and upset. She repeated over and over again: "What did I do??? I didn't do anything! Why won't you talk to me??" I just didn't have the words and if she didn't see what was wrong I wasn't going to waste the time telling her.

I pull up to her house and I ask her to get her bags, exit my vehicle and never call me again. She just sat there. I repeated myself and added a please at the end. She just sat there. I got out of the truck walked around tried to get her out, she'd lock the door. I'm thinking at this point: It's late, I could have left you where you were, and I just want to be left alone. I got back in the truck and ask her for a final time to exit the vehicle. I thought about calling the police but I didn't want to have to wait.

Now I turn and I just sit. The more I sat, the madder I got. She reached across and clicked her seatbelt as if to say she's not going anywhere. I reached across to take the seat belt off of her because I'd had enough. She fought me the entire time, scratching, pulling and hitting.

I couldn't take anymore. I drew back with my free hand and punched her right in the eye. Needless to say all actions stopped after that.

She just sat there holding her eye. I was terrified. First thought, I'm going straight to jail.

I started my truck and went back to my apartment. I sat there for a few minutes. I wanted to die. I couldn't believe I hit her and I couldn't believe she pushed me to that point. After I accepted that fact that the ball was in her court, I asked her to call the police and get it over with. She didn't. I started my truck and we went up to my apartment. I made several ice packs for her to put on her eye. It looked horrible. I think I cried more than she did. I had never hit a woman. Never thought I would have to.

Still in my mind, I'm going to jail. It's only a matter of time. But no… She stayed at my place for a few days until the swelling went down and used makeup to cover up the discoloration. I felt terrible and tried to make sense of it all time and time again. Once the dust settled on the entire incident, we kind of just faded out. She wanted to continue on and asked me if I still loved her and I just couldn't. Too much disrespect was displayed. I apologized profusely for what I had done but she did own the part she part played in it as well. She apologized and we've since moved on.

Chapter XIV: The Story of Sabrina & Paris

After getting fed up with the dating scene in the DC area, I wanted to meet/date women from another zip code, city, country even. There was a world of women that I hadn't explored. I was tired of the pretentiousness of some of the women in the area, the feeling of entitlement. I wanted someone that would appreciate me and who and I am a man. All I've ever wanted was to feel appreciated.

I met Sabrina through a mutual friend on social media. She was a beautiful younger southern belle with a lot of potential. Even with the age difference, we hit it off instantly. She lived in Tennessee and the company I worked for had some work there in the upcoming month.

Excited at the thought of seeing one another, we would use Google Video to stay in touch and see one another. I have to admit I was totally smitten, it felt like high school again. What I enjoyed most about talking to her was her southern accent and her innocence. When I say innocence I mean she hadn't yet been jaded by any of life's experiences. I didn't have to fight through layers of hurt, deceit, guilt, regret, etc. that a lot of women are carrying about. So talking to a woman that wasn't so guarded was refreshing.

We met in July of 2012 and I was supposed to head to Tennessee for work in late August. So we had a month before we would meet in person. In addition to the work I had out of town, my company would host a yearly offsite to a remote location for its employees. The offsite was time for the company to get away from work and celebrate family. There was an awards banquet was well to celebrate the accomplishments of the company as a whole and to recognize people that went above and beyond to make the company look good.

The offsite trip was a two weeks before the trip to Tennessee. I receive a call from the wife of a friend of mine (at the time) that worked for the same company as I did and she ask me if I was going to the offsite alone and I told her yes. She proceeded to ask me if I would mind if Paris went to the offsite as my guest.

Paris and I have a very brief history. Long story short, I was interested in dating Paris at one point. She let me know that she was just getting out of a situation and she doesn't date friends of her brother. Understandable, so we remained really good friend. She knew about Sabrina and she was happy for me.

I let my co-worker know that it was ok for Paris to go. Now... This is my thinking. I'm entertaining Sabrina but I'm attracted to Paris. Paris and I will be sharing a room. I won't make any moves that aren't made on me. That's my story and I'm sticking to it.

We all drive up to the offsite. We had a ball. It was a great little road trip. Meanwhile in Tennessee, Sabrina and her girls are preparing for a girls trip to Jamaica. We even talk over Google Video while I'm at the offsite and she's in Jamaica. All is going well Friday night. Paris and I chill and talk about a little bit of everything until we both fell asleep.

Saturday was a totally different story. Paris was a little more flirty that usual which was welcomed but puzzling. That evening was the Employee banquet. I got dressed first and headed to the ball room. Sat down at my table and I'm still trying to process the flirting from earlier. Why me? Why now?

I look over toward the entrance and she walked in… Paris had on what I like to call "The Dress". It was my favorite color, red, and fit her body like a glove. I knew I was in trouble and lots of it. The evening goes on and we're both flirting, making eyes, etc. I got up to head to the front of the resort for some fresh air. I decided right at that moment I was going to sleep on the patio. Soon as I completed that thought, my phone rang… It was Paris.

She wanted to know where I was and why I left her alone. I couldn't believe this was happening. Why don't people want you when you want them? She knows I have someone, why would she put me in this position? All types of thoughts ran through my head. Anyway, I let her know that I just stepped out for a few and I was on the front porch of the resort. She asked me why I left her, I didn't have a response. When she asked if I was coming back, I said no and that I was headed back to the room. She then let me know that she would be heading back to the room too. I just said ok and held the phone.

There were tons of emotions there, way too many for me to process. I kind of felt like I was cheating on Sabrina but we had never even met. How could I commit to that? I had no idea what Sabrina was doing in Tennessee or Jamaica. So again, how could I commit to something when there are so many unknown variables?

I get back to the room and Paris is not too far behind me. She walked in the room; I'm seated in the corner. She smiles. I smile. One thing leads to another and we have "our moment". Even afterward I'm still in didn't believe what happened. The next day it was business as usual. I have my morning talk with Sabrina over Google Video and we're both packing to head back to DC.

Paris and I continue to see one another but not for long. As my trip to Tennessee approaches, Paris asked me if I'm still going to see Sabrina. I told her yes. Don't think that's the answer she wanted to hear but it was the truth. I'm not going to stop my good thing because you now decide that you want to be with me. Not going to happen. She asked me to choose between her and Sabrina because she didn't want to be led on. Without breaking eye contact I told her that I chose Sabrina.

With that situation in the rear view, I could focus on my situation with Sabrina. We finally meet in Tennessee in person and we just clicked. She was just as beautiful in person, smart, funny and hospitable. The week I spent there was incredible and I wanted more.

Her birthday was in September and I flew her into DC for her birthday. I laid out the red carpet if I do say so myself. Her favorite color, purple. I found purple roses. I went to the grocery store and bought all her favorite things. Her gifts were pretty impressive as well. I wanted her to have the best birthday ever. She heads back to Tennessee one happy woman.

So the plan is for us to see one another once a month. I was set to go to Tennessee to stay with her. Work had been hectic so I was happy to get out of town. When I got to Tennessee, I didn't feel like I got the same reception she got. Now I didn't do all I did to get anything in return but I do expect the same treatment when I come to your city. That didn't happen.

The disappointment of that trip and some other things that happened on her end lead to believe she might not be ready to be with me. Not that I'm better that this or that, I just have standards and from what I've been told pretty high ones. I don't think they're too high, but I will call someone on the carpet if the standard isn't met. No point in having a standard or rule you don't enforce.

I cut back communications with Sabrina a lot after that visit. Her friend reached out because I wouldn't talk to her. I didn't feel like I should have to say anything. You knew the standard and you gave me what you wanted. So I have nothing to say.

After her friend pleaded with me to at least speak with her, I did. I gave have a chance to get the closure she needed on things. I never said what she did wrong. I didn't feel the need to. I was supposed to go to Tennessee for Thanksgiving but since things were on the outs with Sabrina it was likely what I wouldn't.

At the top of November, my job let me know that they would be terminating my position at the top of the year and I needed to look for a job. I had been there 5 ½ years and I was crushed. My job was the one thing I depended on to be there is it was going away. Without love, at least I could focus on work. I can't even do that now.

I tell Sabrina the news and she supportive. She asked me if I was coming to Tennessee for Thanksgiving. I told her I had to hold onto every dime because I didn't know how long it would take for me to find a job. She offered to pay for gas from DC to Tennessee and back if I still wanted to come. I did want to see her and I needed to drive to clear my head and work on my next career move so I took Sabrina up on her offer.

She sent me the money for gas and I headed out. I had a lot time to think on able of things during that 10 hour drive. I pulled up in the wee hours of the morning on Thanksgiving. Tired from the trip, I don't even bring my bags in. I come in a sit down and I noticed her adjustments right away. Everything I had an issue with, she corrected. Without a word from me.

I was highly impressed. The next morning she made breakfast and we had a long talk. I explained to her that I had been through a lot in life and I'm not in the position to take any losses. I give until I can't give anymore with nothing in return. I have to start getting a return on my investment. Not monetarily, but in action and in deed. I commended her on her efforts and thanked her. I asked her if she wanted to give us another try, she replied yes.

So with love getting back on course and employment still a huge question mark, I decided to start that non-profit I had been talking about. L.I.F.E. Starts Here Mentoring Program. The mentorship program was designed to help young people navigate the water of life and inform them as much as possible about becoming an adult and living life to the fullest.

I took my last bit of saving to start that the mentoring program hoping that it would take right off away but that didn't happen. I've learned that there is a process to everything including in the non-profit world.

It's now December and she's slated to come here for Christmas. Since things were going so well again we talked about her moving to DC. I was very excited about her moving here to be with me. It meant the world to me that she trusted me enough to make such a major move for us.

In my head, I didn't want her to move to DC as my girlfriend or fiancé. If she was going to move I wanted her to have more of a promise as my wife. She later expressed to me that she felt pressured into marrying me but that was never my intent. I wanted her to move for something solid. Nothing more, nothing less.

I did share with Sabrina about my accident and mental illness diagnosis. What I didn't share with her was how or when I go through depression. After finding out about my job letting me go, I started to self-medicate. I hated the way bipolar meds made me feel with a passion and I had to find a fix to feel better so that I could be function.

Since depression makes me sleep, I needed something that could keep me awake. I started to run in a few different circles that had access to what I needed to feel better. I tried just about any and every "pleasure drug" to feel better. I smoked a lot of weed and played around with cocaine. Cocaine actually ended up being my favorite but I knew better than to do too much. Throw in some ecstasy and it was a party every day.

I flew Sabrina here for Christmas and while she was here we got married at the courthouse with plans of doing a wedding in 2013. I think she could sense that something wasn't right but she never said anything. I tried to mask my habits as best I could but it was only a matter of time before it would be noticeable.

After her trip in December, we were scheduled to go on a ski trip with some friends of mine. Sometime before that though, I called Sabrina and tripped out. I was high as a kite off of something and I told her about the "affair" with Paris. She was extremely disappointed and pissed off. I apologized to her and she forgave me as best she could. I know she would never fully forgive me. All I could do was spent the rest of my life trying to make it up to her.

January comes and it's time for the ski trip. She flies here and we drive up to the mountains. Things aren't perfect but we're working at getting through. I'm still self-medicating but less now because it's getting close to time for her to move to DC. Her being in DC would have been great motivation and I needed her to stay away from using drugs to feel better. We enjoy ourselves on the ski trip and she heads back to Tennessee to prepare for her move to DC.

February is upon us and it's time for Sabrina to move to DC. I fly there to help her pack and everything. She's quit her job; throw furniture away, given furniture away, etc. She's ready to go. During that week, she began to have these moments. She talked about all the people she said she would miss, missing Tennessee and more. Not really in my right frame of mind because of all I have going on, I flip out on her. I start yelling and cursing talking about her changing her mind and wanting to abandon me. She said nothing of the sort. She was merely expressing that she's making a huge move and she needed me to be there and understand as much as I could. She needed my comfort, my reassurance that everything would be ok.

After things calmed down, she told me that she wasn't moving. She said that I really scared her with my rant and she didn't feel comfortable moving. Still way too emotional to deal with that, I demand to be flown home. She finds the money to fly me home. I cried the entire flight home. I knew for a fact it was over.

Once I get back to DC, I went into 'Operation Salvage' and try to fix what's really the unfixable. I tried for months to get her to change her mind and she wouldn't. After months of asking, pleading I had to accept that it was over. I didn't want to accept it not even because of her. I didn't want to accept the failure of yet another marriage.

I fought her on the divorce for a while and did more to get on her nerves than I did to fix anything. I learned a lot from that situation. This divorce probably hurt the worse because I really wanted it be her. I wanted Sabrina to be the last and final chapter. The most important thing I learned, you can't force anything in life. Anything you have to force, it's not for you and you're asking for trouble. What and who is for you is just that, for you.

My sincerest prayer is that everyone who reads this book takes something good from it. I've had to overcome a lot in my life as I'm sure all of you have. But some of you are still bound by the decisions of your past. It is important to first forgive yourself and ask for forgiveness. Addressing these two areas are very important before moving onto the next relationship.

Here are a few things that helped me to become whole again:

Ownership – I had to get to the point where I "owned my stuff", the good and the bad. No one is as great as we think they are and no one is as bad as we think they are. This goes for us as well. Take ownership of your shortcomings and address them as best you can. Don't beat yourself up over the mistakes, everyone makes them. Also, celebrate and acknowledge the good things about yourself. We're all still learning and growing every day. Be balanced and be blessed.

Accountability – Be accountable for the things you say and the things you do. This goes hand and hand with ownership. Accountability can help you create a baseline for action. It's like keeping your own personal scorecard so you'll know what areas you're strong and the areas you can improve.

Integrity – Integrity is doing the right thing(s) when no one is watching. Integrity is doing the right thing and sometimes there nothing in it for you to gain. A lot of people are motivated by what's in it for them. Sometimes it's just to make the other person in your life happy. Practice operating with integrity and remember that it's a process. Sometimes all the reward you need is knowing you've done the right thing.

Chapter XV: Lessons Learned: Being a Man | Being a Husband

Being a Man

Lesson #1: A man without a plan is a man that plans to fail.

Lesson #2: If you do not lead, you eventually end up being led.

Lesson #3: You don't need to experience a thing to understand a thing. Learn from the lessons of others.

Lesson #4: The more information you have, the better decisions you can make.

Lesson #5: You can't put a price on Integrity.

Being a Husband

Lesson #1: Little gestures go a long way.

Lesson #2: The same things you did to get her, do those things to keep her.

Lesson #3: Compliment her often.

Lesson #4: Being a Gentleman will never go out of style.

Lesson #5: Time spent is better than money spent.

There were plenty of days when I wanted to give up on love. This composition by Jill Scott helped me tremulously through those tough times. Thank you Ms. Scott for such an awesome arrangement.

Here My Call - Jill Scott

Here I am again asking questions,

Waiting to be moved... I am so unsure of my perception,

What I thought I knew I don't seem to

Where is the turn so I can get back to

what I believe in?

Back to the old me and...

God, please hear my call, I am afraid for me.

Love has burned me raw I need your healing

Please... Please... Please

I am such a fool

How did I get here?

Played by all the rules

Then they changed

I am but a child to your vision

Standing in the cold and rain

Lost here in the dark

I can't see.

My foot to take a step, what is happening?

Oh, this hurts so bad.

I can hardly breathe.

I just want to leave so...

God, please hear my call. I am afraid for me.

Love has burned me raw I need your healing...

Please.

God, please hear my call. I am afraid.

Love has turned me cold I need you healing

Please... Please... oh Please... please... oh... oh

God, please hear my call. I am afraid for me.

Love has turned me cold I need your healing

Please... Please... please

please... please... please

Closing Prayer

This prayer is for the women referred to in this project…

Dear Heavenly Father,

I thank you for each and every encounter with the women mentioned in these writings. I appreciate them for accepting me where I was in life and loving me anyway. I ask for forgiveness for anything that I took and I ask that you restore it all 100 fold. I ask that you heal, that you bring them joy and happiness. I ask that you give them an extra measure of favor in anything they pursue and give them their hearts desire. I ask for forgiveness for any pain I caused and tears I caused.

I'm a better man from each situation and I pray that are better women

as well. I pray for their safety, their peace and prosperity. Thank you

God for being in the midst of it all and thank you for your grace,

your mercy and everlasting love…

Amen

A Letter to my Future Wife

I am often asked if I would ever marry again and my response is

always the same, yes. The problem isn't the union of marriage; it's the two people in the union. I believe the woman that's for me is out there and with that I would like to end this project with a letter to her in the off chance that she will have purchased this book:

I'd like to first thank you for purchasing this book. There was a lot of information covered in this reading and it's a lot to digest, I know, but it was my journey to you. These pages are but a glance into the depth of who I am as a man and husband. With that said, I make the following promises:

1. I promise to never run away from our problems.

2. I promise to respect you and your opinion as my partner.

3. I promise to always be open and honest about my feelings.

4. I promise to always tell you the truth no matter the issue big or small.

5. I promise to do my best to maintain the love we have for one another.

I look forward to meeting you and spending the rest of my life with you...

Until then,

Taijuan E. Gales

Special Thank You's

Tynetta Ali - the best accountant on the planet

Michael Rogers - awesome advice and inspiration

Zorana L. Clanton - prayers and motivation

Credits

Book Cover Art

Tony Lux

Book Photograph

Tony Lux

Edits

Zorana Clanton

Lisa Venus

Made in the USA
Columbia, SC
03 July 2018